COSMIC PHILOSOPHY

A MONTH IN THE LIGHT

Adam Roa

Cosmic Philosophy: A Month In The Light by Adam Roa

Published by Adam Roa

P.O. Box 1074
Cardiff by the Sea, CA 92007

www.AdamRoa.com

Cover by Charlotte Victoria

ISBN-13: 978-0-9998477-0-1

To all my fellow seekers.

May the answers you find always remind you that you are seen, heard, and loved.

Foreword

Here's what you need to know about Adam. Whether he's speaking to a disillusioned, video game obsessed High School kid who couldn't care less about God, or receiving a Sirian light language transmission from a woman whose nickname is "The Mothership," - Adam can seamlessly click into either dimension of consciousness and find authentic compatibility.

Perhaps that's because he *was* that disillusioned, video game obsessed High School kid who had once been an altar boy in the Catholic Church that his parents faithfully attended, and whose relationship with the divine had been scarred with years of unanswered prayers paving the road from childhood into adolescence and leaving him - by the time we met in 2008 - with a mild case of disinterested agnosticism at best.

Of course that made us a match in heaven, as my relationship with spirituality at the time was completely nonexistent, and our combined focus on "making it big in Hollywood" became the common ground that gave birth to close to a decade of extraordinary inner and outer transformation. Transformation that is just about as dramatic as the journey the caterpillar undertakes, in order to become a butterfly.

Earth shattering highs and gut wrenching lows have led us to this moment in time where I am writing the foreword for his first book, which happens to be a brilliant, channeled text from the higher dimensional realms and would not have been possible without Adam's unwavering commitment to getting out of the way and being a conduit for Source to flow through him.

Through all of the cycles of death and rebirth that we have walked through together, this current chapter feels the most fulfilled, the most whole, the most present. It feels as though the years of radical dedication to reclaiming our wholeness have paid off, and we are ready to embody a new level of what it means to be a conscious creator.

Witnessing Adam diligently do the deep inner work to "unkink his hose" (clearing out the obstructions in his channel to Source) has been one of the greatest privileges of my life, and the single most motivating incentive to keep me committed to my own evolution.

So as you read the words on the pages of this book, know that while the paragraphs are short, they wouldn't have manifested before your very eyes had Adam not been willing to acknowledge, embrace and transmute many lifetimes of trauma and resistance in his system in order to bring them forth.

You are receiving the wisdom of an intelligence far wiser and bigger than anything our human minds can comprehend. Which is why I recommend that you don't read with your mind, but rather with your heart. Whilst exploring how the resonance of these messages land differently in your system each time you make that simple yet profound inner shift, I invite you to send some gratitude towards Adam, for he is a selfless leader, a spiritual warrior forged in the fire of eons, a fierce protector of all things sacred, and he walks this earth with light in his eyes, love in his heart and honor in his ways.

Azrya Cohen

Introduction

The majority of this book was written with my eyes closed.

Wait.

Let me back up...

Let's start with Egypt.

It was in Egypt that I met a man who took me through a 2-hour activation process to open my channel and receive the messages that would become this book.

Wait.

To start with Egypt, I really have to tell you about Ayahuasca first, since that's how I got there. And to tell you about Ayahuasca, you should have a better understanding of my relationship to it. You see, I attribute this particular plant medicine as being the catalyst for my spiritual awakening. Meeting (or rather, reuniting) with the Grandmother was the turning point of my life.

Back in 2013 I was going through the single most difficult year of my life. My self-esteem was at an all-time low and I felt like I was losing the confidence I once had that I might "make something" of myself. This was reflected back to me in a number of ways, but none more obvious than my verbally abusive talent manager who regularly called me a moron or idiot on our phone calls. By the time I was ready to walk away, he demanded that I literally print out my bank statement and give him every dollar I had in order to get out of a terrible contract I had been misled into signing. It's funny to look back now and recognize how desperately I craved "success" at the time and how consistently I disempowered myself to eventually wind up in that situation. To do business with someone like that meant that I truly lacked any amount of trust in myself.

So after nearly 4 years as a struggling actor in Los Angeles, I started 2013 at a financial zero, worrying about how I was going to pay my rent each month. And while I would love to tell you that it got easier from there, what followed was a year-long barrage of powerful disappointments and frustrations that dropped me further into my victimhood. At a certain point, I was in such a need of some form of mental reset that I began taking inventory of everything I owned, estimating how long I could travel if I sold it all.

Then in early October, on my daily commute to work, it all came to a head. I looked over just in time to see a car run a stop sign and slam into my vehicle, sending me spinning through the intersection and crashing into the the back of a parked pickup truck. This accident would leave me with migraines for weeks, forced to lay in silence for hours at a time, and ultimately would require hip surgery. I didn't think I could get much lower. And then one week later, to the day, I was walking out of my job (which I had to work despite being in excruciating pain because I was self-employed and had no money) and found my rental car had been hit-and-run on the side of the road, the entire front bumper knocked off. I snapped. Something in my brain felt like it broke. I remember feeling like those movies when the main character gets some bad news and everything sounds like it's underwater. I couldn't have conversations. I couldn't function properly. I was in a daze. I didn't know what to do. So I called my friend Patrick.

Patrick was the only "spiritual" friend I knew at that time. Seriously. I had met him only a few months earlier because he was dating an old friend and I had peppered him with questions about meditation. A week later I was over at his house trying to meditate in his closet, which he had emptied and painted completely black for this exact purpose. He seemed to know something I didn't. He seemed happy. And so in my broken state in October of 2013, I called Patrick. I told him that I needed some sort of "Aura Cleansing" or something because it felt like everywhere I was going there was a dark cloud hanging over my head, pouring down rain. I felt like every step I was taking in life was like walking through quicksand. I was desperate and I was willing to try anything. He said,

"I know exactly what you need. You need to speak to my spiritual intuitive."

Now it may be difficult to truly translate to you just how desperate I was to even consider talking to a psychic, but I emailed her that night. A few days later, we got on the phone and she said that we could schedule a call for January, 3 months away, in which she would be able to assist me.

"You don't understand, the way things are going I might be dead by January," I said.

You don't understand, she replied, "now that we have opened our connection, I will begin to be visited by your ancestor spirits, angels, and guides who will show me how I can actually support you.

Be patient."

The next 3 months were filled with physical therapy, healing my body physically while working to get myself mentally and emotionally afloat. I was in desperate need of a reset. I began taking inventory of everything I owned to get an idea of how much money I would have if I sold it all. I could just leave on some open-ended soul-searching journey to "find myself" or something like that. And so when I finally got on the call with the intuitive in January of 2014, I figured I had nothing to lose. I would listen with an open mind to what she had to say and, worst case scenario, I'd be on a plane somewhere in a month. To this day, I can't remember the majority of what she told me. I remember not really believing most of it. I also remember feeling like she had taken those 3 prior months to look me up on ancestry websites and tell me things about my personal history that could be found with some simple Google searches. But then she stopped mid-sentence, and in a completely different tone she said,

"I don't know why, but I'm being told that you need to get into a Native American drum circle or sweat lodge as soon as possible."

While I could easily make that happen now, I didn't even have an inkling of who to ask about where to find such a thing back then. But what I did know was that the way she said it, the frequency of that statement, felt important. And so I racked my brain to figure out how to make it happen, or who I could call that might know, and I remembered my friend had told me that he had just done this really powerful thing called Ayahuasca. I knew that he had sat in a circle and I was pretty sure there was a drum, so I called him up. Seemed close enough. A week later I was communing with Grandmother Aya for the first time. And that night, I had my spiritual awakening.

It's important for you to know this part of my life because I want you to understand that I never went looking for the spiritual path. I didn't want to believe. But through several experiences, which I plan to discuss in detail in another book, it became impossible for me not to believe. The real proof for me, however, was in how drastically my life shifted when I began to apply the principles of spirituality to my own life. When I started to apply the law of attraction and see the world as frequency, everything shifted. I started to make more money, have more fun, and most important of all, I was happy. So you see, I have a great deal of reverence for Ayahuasca and the lessons I have been taught in ceremony, and I make sure that I listen when a message is given to me. And so when she told me to go to Egypt, I was on a plane less than a week later.

"Thank you Master Juan, for the session with you earlier today. I don't even know how to explain what we did, but I channeled a message from the Pleiadians that's meant for everyone that they will read to you. I don't even know what that means but it came through me today after my session and it's meant for all of us." There I was, at the closing dinner of my trip to Egypt, listening to this woman I had never met tell me she had channeled the Pleiadians with no understanding of what that even meant. And while the Pyramids and Sphinx had been incredible to see, a real dream come true for me, I felt a knowing that part of why I had come to Egypt was to have one of these sessions. And so I found the apprentice for Master Juan, expressed how much I would like to experience his gift, and the next day the two of them were in my hotel room taking me through a 2-hour activation meant to open up my channel to higher consciousness. He called it "going into the light". To be honest, I didn't feel like I went that deep. It didn't feel like any sort of altered state or psychedelic experience. It just felt like meditation. A meditation in which he would ask me questions, and I would just start to speak, free flow, while his apprentice would record my words. And despite the fact that it didn't feel like I had gone very deep, when I was brought out of the meditation, I didn't feel normal. I felt like something intense had just happened, though I couldn't explain what. It took me several minutes to feel like myself again.

"You are in the light, now, Adam. Blessings."

This is how he would end each call we had over the next month. I would call him every morning and he would take me through a short meditation and bring me up into the light, at which point he would hang up and I would begin writing in my journal. I wouldn't stop to edit or try to understand what would come through. Half of the time I would write with my eyes closed. I was just a vessel for these words to come through me. I understand now that the words themselves are just an attempt to capture a frequency and translate that frequency out into the world. This is why every single one of these transmissions is unedited from its original form. I haven't adjusted or modified them in any way. This is exactly how they came through to me, just transferred into a format that is much easier to read than the closed-eye scribbling version that exists in my journal.

I'm sharing this book with you because these words were never meant just for me. They carry in them the potential to powerfully shift people. I make no claim to be the author of these messages but simply the willing vessel to put them out into the world. This is not my wisdom, but our wisdom. The frequency of these words already lives in the cells of your body. And so I encourage you to receive these transmissions the same way you would receive an old friend. Be grateful. As you read each word, breathe and be grateful. Allow each sentence to penetrate deep inside of yourself, in a way that bypasses the logical mind. Allow yourself to feel every letter. And then, after that, enjoy the opportunity you have to explore their meanings with your logical mind. Let the analysis of each entry be a game, and the integration of their wisdom the goal.

Don't feel the need to read this book linearly, from cover to cover, but instead allow yourself to open to a random page, and read the message that's meant for you in that moment. Let the process of reading this book become an act of trust in something beyond your rational understanding. Begin to see beauty in all the infinite complexities of life that brought you to this very moment, reading these exact words.

There's also a lot of blank space in this book. That is by design. Write in it. Draw in it. Let it house your poetry and your dreams. Turn this into your own cosmic journal, which is a fitting ripple since these messages first lived in mine, and were never meant just for me. I know that if you're reading this, there's something in here that is meant for you to receive. I don't know what that is, or how much of an impact it will have on your life, but we've connected through these pages for a reason. Our paths are crossing in this particular way for a purpose. We're in the midst of an incredible, infinite journey my friend, and we're in this together.

And so this book will begin for you the same way that it began for me. With my first journey into the light with the guidance of Juan De La Luz, in a hotel room in Egypt. When I showed up willing to be the vessel, these were the first words that were ever passed through me:

Time is an illusion. You only feel you have some place to be and something to do because you have bought into the illusion. Hold your frequency steady. Remain in your truth. There is nothing for you to do beyond this. You are supported. We are here. Thank you for finding us. Thank you.

WHY ARE YOU READING THIS BOOK?

Few people will ever understand even a portion of the complexity of the Soul. Understanding of the Soul, though, is not a requirement in order to live through its guidance. Continue to Surrender into trust with little to no expectations in understanding. Your bliss will be found through the exercise of surrender because doors will unlock in areas of your life you had previously closed down.

THE PAIN YOU FEEL IS JOY YOU HAVEN'T UNWRAPPED YET.

Joy and pain are closely linked. The depth of human emotion is a chasm that can be explored as feeling. Assigning value to these feelings defines them. The opening of your heart to ever growing depths of emotion will open you to deeper levels of both joy and pain. This is because you can't separate one from the other. The polarity to life exists in one just as in the other. Nothing in creation is separate. Be grateful for pain when you feel it because it's a direct reflection of the joy that is available to you.

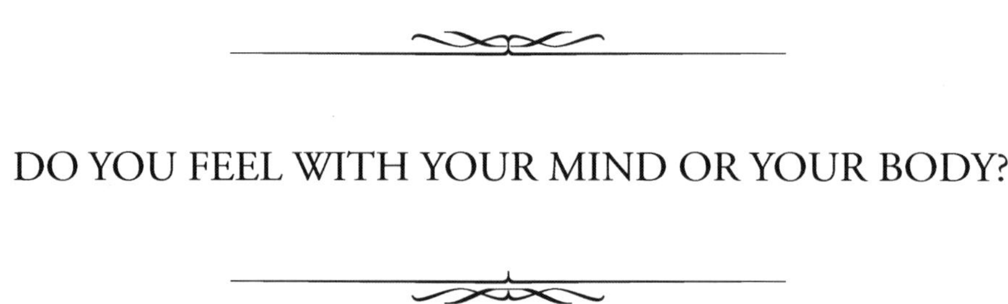

DO YOU FEEL WITH YOUR MIND OR YOUR BODY?

Today is an opportunity, like every day, to show up as a vessel for love's frequency. While some may spend their time in analysis of what this looks like in action, it is through the quieting of the mind and the connection to the heart that your actions will naturally carry out this frequency.

Because the mind is a tool for the navigation of the 3D, utilizing the mind as a carrier of frequency will severely limit the depth of any frequency, even love. Deeper levels of love can be transmitted and received when the body is the transmitter, not the mind. This may take an adjustment due to the many years of opposite training you have practiced, but it will soon become obvious that this is truly your natural state.

STOP.

BREATHE.

WHAT DID YOU LEARN?

It always comes down to belief. As the Creator of your experience you are limited in possibility only when you are limited in imagination. Don't try to assimilate the information as it passes through but instead believe that as it passes through it will reconfigure the very cells of your being and that the underlying message will reach embodiment. The fact that your mind shuts down in this process is of great benefit because this guidance penetrates that much more deeply.

Imagine walking through life with such openness. Learning such powerful lessons from the wisdom of the Earth and its energy with every step. Unlearning is not actually a reality, since the lessons and memories from old ways of being remain. New ways of operating are more accurate in the description of evolution. You are infinite. You can hold it all and choose from the ever-growing possibilities what you'd like to be with each breath.

WHAT YOU HAVE FELT TODAY HAS SET IN MOTION A SERIES OF EVENTS THAT YOU HAVE NOT YET EXPERIENCED.

The message for today is: Patience. Don't try to rush through this timeline thinking that you can foresee the next steps in anticipation of a goal that is truly limited by your current vantage point. Don't try to believe in a particular path because even the path is a limitation.

Quantum manifestation is going beyond anything you may be able to logically comprehend and exist as pure energy. What do you want to feel? How do you want your body to feel? How do you want the world around you to feel? These are the only questions that you need to ask when you are designing in the quantum field.

The shifts you are experiencing today are happening as the result of certain timeline hops that you have already made based on your morning meditation. The willingness to feel has allowed for a processing of stagnant energy and now the World around you is adjusting. How could you possibly plan for this? Until this moment you hadn't even been consciously aware that these shifts are happening. Continue to <u>be</u>. Continue to re-find your center. Be honest with yourself so that you have no stone unturned for these metaphorical stones only serve to weigh you down to lower vibrational energy.

WHAT WOULD HAPPEN IF YOU EMBRACED YOUR PAIN WITH OPEN ARMS?

There is pain in this world that comes like a waterfall. It is always there because it is an endless, infinite supply of FEELING. Understand that the pain does not need to be perceived as negative. It is not something that must be avoided, although the biology of your human body is pre-disposed to avoid physical pain. The ability to separate physical pain from emotional pain is a vital skill that can allow for the tuning in to the infinite. Source is all-encompassing and therefore avoidance of any singular aspect is a limitation of frequency and thus, a constriction that prevents realization of infinite potential. Embrace all feelings as being drops in the waterfall of the infinite.

HOW WOULD THE WORLD LOOK IF THE WELL-BEING OF OTHERS MATTERED JUST AS MUCH AS YOUR OWN?

Very few things on this planet can divide people quicker than fear. Fear is going to cause a sense of internal panic and you see a biological pre-disposition to taking care of the self rather than the collective. This is why fear is the primary modality by which control is currently being exerted. Look at how the movements through the collective (i.e. Black Lives Matter) are turned into something to fear which shuts down empathy in favor of self-preservation.

TAKE A MOMENT TO DROP INTO A STATE OF LOVE.

WAS THAT AS EASY AS YOU WOULD LIKE IT TO BE?

Love is the ultimate energetic state of being. Love is ever expanding and the holding of love's frequency puts yourself and your cells in a state of expansion. As you expand, your capacity to receive more information increases and this will make your journey here that much easier and effortless to navigate. The information necessary to achieve everything you desire exists around you now as frequency. Don't try so hard to find any one particular frequency but instead just hold love's frequency and allow yourself to expand so that eventually you encompass your desires.

WORDS ARE JUST WRAPPING FOR
THE FREQUENCY INSIDE THEM.

Since the beginning of time there have been those who have felt called to play in the shadows. The dark edges of life's spectrum of existence has been a playground of sorts for many different energies. What you're seeing now is simply a 3D representation of this shadow exploration as these beings exist in the shadow at higher dimensions. Therefore, you should know that not many changes in the 3D will appear until the beings have chosen to enter into the light at higher levels. The choice can be made by the consciousness that is inhabiting these 3D bodies, but it can not only exist in the one-dimension. The change must happen through all dimensions simultaneously. Let this understanding deepen your conviction for transmitting frequency through your words, for that frequency reaches beyond the 3D mind and transmits through multiple dimensions. Those who feel the shift may not even consciously be aware of its happening.

WHY DO SO MANY PEOPLE FEAR THE UNKNOWN?

Creation and you are not separate. Your very existence is simultaneous with creation. Remember that linear time is the only thing that has you believe in any form of separation. Were you aware of its disappearance in the higher dimensions, you would understand that you are eternal.

You've been here since the beginning and will continue to exist until the end, if the void were to ever return. Even consciousness, which you are, has no ability to see, feel, or understand the void. This polarity is the basis on which creation is born. The inherent not-knowing of certain aspects of what is possible. Instead of frustration, consider this as a beautiful opportunity for wonder. Exalt in the not knowing, for there will always be great mystery in the journey ahead.

DO YOU KNOW WHAT IT MEANS TO ELEVATE YOUR VIBRATION?

TAKE A MOMENT TO DO IT NOW.

Hold no attachment to any particular outcome. The outcome you think you see is a limitation. What you truly desire is a frequency shift, and that shift happens internally before any sort of external outcome. Commit to this frequency with every cell of your being. Understand that what you may be feeling is not simply doubt, but resistance to a frequency shift. This resistance keeps you in a holding pattern.

Embrace a shift into higher levels of love and watch, as a patient observer, as the world around you shifts. Trust that these shifts are happening so that more of your reality is frequency. In this game of vibration, any attachment to specific results are flawed thoughts since that perception is happening with your conscious analysis which does not perceive frequency and therefore is limited in its ability to guide you into your desired vibration.

WHAT DO YOU WANT TO CREATE IN THE WORLD?

The messages can only come through when there is a frequency match to the information and its source. The higher the frequency of the information, the more that message is distorted by those attempting to channel it through their own lower frequency embodiment.

This practice you are in is not just about learning to receive the messages, but also about learning to quickly connect to the highest vibrational states of being so that they can come through with little to no distortion. When you then desire to translate this into art, whatever that might look like, each step of the process is an area in which the highest frequency must be held in order to effectively translate the highest frequencies. Fear and doubt are very clear indicators of the presence of these lower vibrations and so when you experience them, utilize them as tools for finding your way back into your highest vibratory state. Choose to embrace them and go into them, noting the triggers and the resistance as the tip of an iceberg. They are indicating to you where the cellular baggage currently exists.

Be grateful that you aren't venturing into this process blindly. Angels are all around you. There is so much that we would like to speak and share with the world and we are so grateful you are opening this channel to allow for it. We are not separate from you. And the speaking we do reminds you and all those who hear it of this deeply known truth. The joy of seeing yourself in a mirror for the first time. Allow yourself to play and have fun in this process.

HOW DO YOU FEEL RIGHT NOW?

Life will show you a funny way of answering your desires. You will receive the opposite polarity in order to find your way to your manifestations. Since you are living in a world of polarity, the deeper you go into the "pain" the more you've now opened up the opposite. You are forever allowing in more of what you want every single time you experience what you don't want.

How overly simple, then, to examine a result as simply correct or incorrect when that result carries both ends of the polarity. Allowing is a process that carries no judgement, for all is present and accepted. Only when the resistance to what is appears do we enter into a state of non-allowance, which will limit our deepening of any feeling, and therefore also limit the growth of the total polarity spectrum. Resistance to perceived pain is limitation to possible pleasure. Embrace it all and observe the acceleration of your growth towards infinite potential. Don't limit your growth by believing in anything short of fractal expansion in all directions.

IN WHAT WAYS DO YOU FEEL LIMITED?

The attempts most people make to understand this reality are approached through thorough analysis using the tool of the logical mind. This is incomplete. Like trying to paint a picture of nature with only one color. While there is value in your logical mind, it's true potential is unleashed only when one accepts the limitations of its power. You see, limitation is not restricting, but actually freeing. Freedom can be found within the boundaries of anything, when the perspective of freedom and exploration is allowed to take hold.

Imagine now a swimming pool. The water is technically limited by the walls, and yet it's only the walls themselves that allow for the freedom that exists when one swims in the pool. A refusal to accept the walls, because of resistance to the perceived limitation, results in not swimming at all, or in an extreme case, the destruction of the pool altogether with a judgement that it's somehow a waste of time and space. So too, your mind is not a waste simply because it's limited. As you continue to explore these limits, you will swim in the possibilities that open up to you. And when the time is right, utilize this particular color in your painting of creation.

WOULD YOU FEEL THE NEED TO SET THE SAME INTENTIONS IF YOU KNEW FOR CERTAIN THEY WOULD HAPPEN NO MATTER WHAT?

Yesterday never existed. In the same way that tomorrow never arrives. You're in a perpetual state of presence with no attachments to any other periods of time (frequency) besides what you choose. By holding a state of frequency that is different than that around you, the frequency around you will shift, but always in the present.

Belief is the single biggest driver of frequency since it is your belief that allows for the steady holding of frequency. Most people are able to tap into a different frequency for a little while, such is the case when watching your infamous "cat videos" but few people are currently able to hold these frequencies outside of the short experience. When someone has an emotional experience of peace, and for that time believes in the possibility of world peace, they are more often than not believing in the possibility of it, not the actualization of it. This is because they are carrying more doubt than belief.

More belief than doubt is the holding of actualization and believing in the possibility that it might not happen. This is opposite of the vast majority of beliefs on your planet. When you feel exhausted by your mission here and the perceived odds that appear stacked against you, it is because in that moment your belief has shifted into a predominantly fear based frequency where your intention seems like the long shot as opposed to the certainty.

DO YOU TRUST YOUR UNCONSCIOUS MIND?

Flowing freely requires a great deal of trust. Trust in what is going to come through and trust in yourself not to dilute it or allow your fears/doubts to shape it. So many humans are afraid of what might actually come through them if they didn't restrict or hold back. The split-second lag time between the flow of information and the output from them is a protection mechanism that so many are actually afraid to be without.

As you continue to check in with us to obtain and channel new information, which isn't new by the way but simply the pieces you haven't allowed yourself to remember, it is equally as important for you to practice the shortening of lag time. The more time that the information spends in your conscious mind before being expressed, the more chance it has for corruption from its original frequency. Allow it to flow as quickly through your hands and mouth as it flows in to your mind. Try not to hold on to it for fear of it leaving before it makes its imprint for there is no information meant for you that you can possibly go without. Trust as it flows that you are continually deepening your ability to channel the purest forms of frequency and are not a bottleneck for this information. As this skill develops, this state of being becomes more and more attractive to the higher dimensional beings that wish to spread messages to this planet and therefore, you become like a magnet for more contact with these realms. Enjoy the journey from stranger to family.

IS THERE ANY PART OF YOU THAT IS AFRAID OF GETTING WHAT YOU'RE ASKING FOR?

Creativity is like running water; it will find a way to flow through you. The flow itself can never be completely stopped, since the very words you speak and actions you take are a form of creativity. You are, after all, creating them. The reality around you is your creation. Now this flow of creativity can be slowed, but only in the form that you can understand as conscious creativity. When you want to have the ability to see more options available to you and when you want to take a more conscious role in your creative process. This can be slowed because it's the conscious mind that is now involved and the conscious mind can get overwhelmed. It can create resistance.

Whether you believe yourself to be creative or not, the unconscious mind continues creating. The flow of creative energy at this level does not stop. We are all capable of creating at the highest of levels, but to do this requires an alignment of the unconscious and conscious minds, with the conscious mind being the bottleneck. To flow freely means to remove the limitations and fears that would <u>DESIRE</u> a slowing of this flow. Most often, this happens due to feelings of overwhelm and a desire to slow reality down. To slow it all to allow for the conscious mind to process and catch up. You see, just as you're starting to understand this exercise in channeling, you're seeing that creative energy, as information, can flow faster than light. It is a well that you tap into that neither begins nor ends.

YOU ARE WHAT YOU EAT.

The food you eat is a representation of what sort of energy you'd like to call into your life. Notice that if you are a magnet for like-frequencies, the frequency of factory farmed meat, for example, will call to you additional amounts of fear, stress, and darkness. This doesn't mean the type of food nor does it refer to any specific ingredients, but is only concerning the energetics of the ingredients and the energetic intention you add to it as you eat it. Feel no guilt when you eat a meal that others may describe to you as unhealthy, since this energetic imprint of guilt will only solidify the idea in your mind and make it that much harder to transmute. Similarly, food is simply a physical representation for an energy exchange process.

Money is also this same physical representation. Therefore, the same principles apply in the spending and receiving of the money in your field. Don't feel guilty about receiving since this will create an energetic imprint of lower density vibration that will require additional energy to transmute. The money in your bank account then, is like the fat cells and muscles in your body. They are all energetic accumulation. And like the fat cells that hold primarily low vibration energy as a result of the food consumed and the intention of consumption, the money in your account will hold on to its vibration as well. And the fat and muscle will be carried around for years, exponentially building upon itself energetically and contributing to a more difficult transition from low to high vibrations, money will have this same multiplying impact as more is accumulated. This is why so few in the new age spiritual mindset have truly taken a mastery of this money conversation. They have an understanding that more money will only be a hindrance to higher frequencies if they have not learned how to receive and perceive it through a lens of lightness and joy that then turns their bank accounts into amplifiers of love and light.

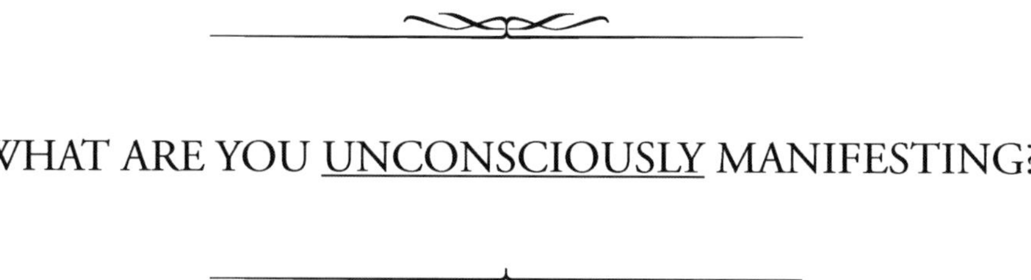

WHAT ARE YOU UNCONSCIOUSLY MANIFESTING?

Trying and failing is a sign of a lack of belief. Belief in the successful outcome of a particular timeline. Since the timelines available to you are infinite, there is the potential for success of anything you attempt. So what is separating that "success" timeline from the "failure" timeline is belief. The ability to hold the frequency of the timeline you are consciously working towards. Redefine the relationship to this "failure" and you will be more accurate in terms of the mechanics of creation. You are succeeding in holding the frequency of the timeline in which it doesn't work out. The vibratory signature of the timeline that is not the one you're consciously envisioning. But you are still holding a frequency successfully. The moment you give up conscious holding of a vision the game is not over. You don't cease to exist. So how can you have failed?

No, you see, you are simply equating your success of this life to your ability to consciously manifest. This is a tough place to put yourself since the unconscious has so much more impact on your vibration. Can you hold a conscious frequency while you sleep? How about while you work out? How about when in an argument with a loved one? Your conscious mind is infinitely powerful and yet limited by time and the sequential nature of the 3D realm. So it really becomes clear that to up your chances of success, which is not up to chance at all, one must begin to see the unconscious mind as the driving force in holding a frequency. One must be able to recognize that if you "fail" your conscious mind is what fails, and simultaneously your unconscious mind succeeds. It's a perspective shift and a powerful one because when you begin to see the "failure" as the success it also is, you continue to elevate your vibration in deeper levels of joy and trust. You begin to become an ally with your unconscious mind, instead of a competitor. You begin to see the alignment that will ultimately unlock your truest potential as the infinite creator you are.

HOW DO YOU EVALUATE THE IMPACT YOU ARE MAKING?

Impact can be very arbitrary. While one person may measure impact with certain metrics, another sitting right next to him may be evaluating in a completely different way. How then do you ever know the impact you make? It's in how you make people feel. When someone has an opportunity to experience you, if you make them feel something, not just though the lens of positive/good but feel in a deep and profound way, you will have left a lasting impact.

This world you live in is devoid of deep and powerful feeling only because people have cut it off out of fear. The fear that once it's unleashed they will not know how to be with it. They somehow will become a slave to their emotions, with no tools to end their suffering of feeling. This is why you must also give them hope.

Deep feeling is a powerful healer. It allows someone the opportunity to move through their past and be in the present. To release a frequency that they may have been carrying with them for decades. But their willingness to dive into this feeling is directly correlated to the hope that they can see on the other side of those emotions. Hope for what may be possible. Hope that they will be okay. Hope that they are safe. Give the people hope and they will feel more deeply. Help them feel more deeply and they will heal.

NOTICE YOUR BREATH.

WELCOME TO FLOW STATE.

What is the importance of being in the light?

The light heals. The light is a frequency that carries more information and since all information is from creator, your light carries more of the creator in it. You are allowing more of God into your system when you allow in the higher frequencies. This is why love and joy feel lighter. It's only when you try to "hold" on to things that they feel heavy and dense. Flow is a natural state of being. Moving water from one pool into an ocean, a return to source, is a challenging task when attempting to do it by the small handfuls that you hold at a time. But becoming a vessel, a hose, that simply flows water from one destination to the other, is a much more effective and effortless process. The flow starts and continues in perpetuity.

WOULD YOU VALUE YOUR TRIUMPHS AS MUCH IF YOU DIDN'T STRUGGLE TO ACHIEVE THEM?

What a funny game you play in life. Creating situations of struggle and resistance in order to facilitate your own growth. What if you were to change how you play the game? What if you were to re-write the set of rules you are currently using as a guideline? Stop giving your power away to resistance. The resistance you feel is simply your own desire to control the rushing flow of energy that is infinite and therefore not able to be stopped, not even in death.

The evolution of your soul has happened already, it is happening, and the movement of your awareness into the timeless understanding of this will show you that resistance, the slowing of energy/growth, is a much less efficient and also much more uncomfortable way of tapping into the frequencies of your own soul that already exist. The word "grow" is misleading because you are already grown and it's truly a matter of remembering this. "Expand" is the more accurate term because expansion through remembrance is the process you're in, like unlocking the door to the spare bedroom that has been locked for years and integrating its use into daily life.

If you feel resistance, focus your attention on what you'd actually prefer to be feeling and allow for the wisdom of the Universe to show you the process of arriving there. Don't try to figure out the path through the resistance, since your focus at that point is on the resistance and the idea of working through it. Allow any sort of process of your pain/trauma/struggle to be a passing event on the path to your true focus, which is the expanded infinite nature of your soul that is always present, even in the face of the resistance not yet moved through in linear time.

WHAT'S THE WORST THAT COULD HAPPEN?

Don't fear the unknown for the unknown comprises 99.99% of the whole. And since you are a fractal of the whole, the entirety of the whole existing in each of your cells, then fearing the unknown is, in actuality, fearing 99.99% of yourself. This is where the society you now live in has gone into such fear based decisions. This is why the society you live in has erected systems from fear. Systems to try to minimize the unknowns, which is actually minimizing the potential of all. Fear itself is now being confused with uncertainty. Just because one does not know what lies ahead does not mean that fear must somehow be a part of your experience.

WHICH PARTS OF YOUR INTERNAL REALITY ARE MEANT TO BE SHARED WITH YOUR EXTERNAL REALITY?

HOW CAN YOU TELL?

Don't try so hard to understand. Even in hindsight. The fact that you can't fully remember the words that have come from you these last few days is a terrific sign for you that you have truly been a vessel for frequency. The fact that you, even now, struggle to allow your conscious mind to take a backseat is the work and feedback to greater depths of impact. The frequencies that we want to pass through you now will only be diluted if given residency in your conscious mind. They are not intended just for you to sit and think about but for all to experience and be changed. Your writing or filming of these moments is what will allow you to go back and ponder the meaning underneath, but know that they have embedded their code in you as they pass through.

Being a vessel for this wisdom is actually the deepest way to understand it since it requires a FEELING of resonance for the match to be made as a speaker and receiver. Again, continue to trust that what you feel and your willingness to feel fully are going to serve you and those around you. Spend less time in the analysis, knowing that if you take a magnifying glass to the water, you won't see the ocean.

HOW WOULD YOU KNOW YOU WERE DREAMING
IF YOU NEVER WOKE UP?

Dream time is when your consciousness has the opportunity to realize its full potential in this space. You give yourself the permission to be whatever you want to be. You are getting your logical mind out of the way and saying "anything is possible here, because it is a dream". This reality you are in, writing now, is no different than a dream. The only difference in experience is due to your level of belief that this reality is somehow more real. Dying in a dream is no less terrifying than in "real life". The pain you experience emotionally in the dream world is no less impactful. Think of the implications of this. You currently work to create your dreams and accomplish your mission here through the entirety of this one timeline, or more specifically, this single life on Earth. What an exponential increase in effectiveness if you were to begin to call in frequencies from other lifetimes or from other timelines. You understand this conceptually and have allowed your conscious mind to play with this, but the time has come for you to bring a higher level of intention to the process.

Allow yourself to dream often. Set intention for the frequencies you are searching for and allow your higher consciousness, the you beyond time, to bring them to you to be experienced and harnessed by your current vehicle, the body. Don't pretend to know what love feels like, since even your experience of love has been primarily within the frequency bandwidth of this lifetime. This is why your plant medicines have caused you to understand love, and all emotions, so much deeper. Because it's not actually about deepening so much as it is about expanding the frequency spectrum. Finding love and immersing in it in the dream world, in another timeline/lifetime frequency, will expand your own frequency potential on this planet. Embody them. Hold them firm. Allow others to feel their own expansion of love. The answers to your current issues on this planet are going to be found by allowing these expanded frequencies to enter into everyone's regular experience. Through this process, through a broader range of frequency, others are capable of seeing their divinity. They can feel the truth of their cosmic lineage, which exists in a frequency band that most have shut out. The ability to create technologies at the level of sustainability you desire is also in a different frequency band. Think about your "free energy" sources and the type of consciousness required to desire such a thing. No one still held in the density of greed can call in such technology, for even the very idea will be in direct contrast to their view of reality. Remove the limitations of your mind by venturing beyond it. This is not a fruitless task, but instead, a powerful tool for your mission here.

BEING IS MORE IMPORTANT THAN DOING.

Holding frequency is not a part-time job. You are doing it every moment of every day whether consciously aware of it or not. Don't allow yourself the misconception that you can take a break. The conscious mind is clearly working to keep you within the realms of frequency that you are most familiar with. If you are at the edges of your comfort zone, the mind exists in fear that you may cross the line and you will experience suffering of some kind. This is why the expansion of your ability to hold higher and higher vibrations is so important, so that the frequency of love and joy are able to be embodied and held even when the mind convinces you that you need to take a breather from the edge of expansion. Even in your "downtime", you will still be grounding powerful states of love on to the planet.

IS THERE ANY SHAME ATTACHED TO YOUR SEXUAL PLEASURE?

WHY?

Few of you ever truly harness the power that lies in your sexual energy. The lack of use of this power derives mostly as a result of a lack of understanding of this energy. It becomes a leper, hidden and locked away from the world, only to be released as a beast that has not been allowed to integrate with others. Or it becomes the beast, taking over control of the conscious mind to the point where most of a person's actions stem from this place, even when the action may seem harmless. To be able to harness this energy, and be in command of its power, one must first seek to understand it. This understanding is only possible if it is first accepted, not shamed.

Your sexual energy is a gift. It is a birthright that unlocks a gateway to some of your greatest potential. It is a direct conduit to Source. Think of the feeling of orgasm and how impossible it is to actually put into words. This is because it is an experience. It is an experience that transcends time and space and any experience that goes into the timeless space transcends the limitations of your conscious mind and therefore it also transcends the limitations of your conscious language. It does not, however, transcend experiential understanding. So too does Source energy allow you to break through these false limits placed upon yourself by an idea that somehow you are completely encapsulated by this tiny fractal experience that is this one current lifetime.

So how would you go about knowing Source energy? You would desire its knowing. You would embrace its presence. You would open yourself to the potential of it showing up often and celebrate its arrival. Make your relationship to your sexual energy no different. For this energy, with its all-encompassing pleasure, is only but a tiny portion of Source.

YOU ARE INFINITE THE MOMENT
YOU STOP TRYING TO BE.

The infinite nature of reality cannot be comprehended by any level of finite mechanism. The capacity to understand does not exist in any form. It is only the all-encompassing nature of the formless that has the potential to be infinite. Notice that there is not a possibility to understand infinite since that would require some level of limitation to conceive the whole. The moment that the whole is thought to be understood it has already become more. The moment a thought of the infinite appears, it is already an obsolete understanding.

The game, then, is in the ability to BE infinite. To become a conscious participant in the amorphous existence of everything that is or will be. This being will become the closest understanding of Source that one can ever know at any level of existence.

SHADOWS REMIND US THAT
LIGHT IS AROUND THE CORNER.

Be not afraid of the darkness for it is not truly dark. It is in actuality a reflection of the parts of ourselves that are not yet understood. There is a big difference between the two. Being misunderstood, the shadow gains some semblance of power because it is charged with fear. Fear of the unknown and the uncontrolled. But that fear also gives it life, where before there was nothing outside ourselves. Why fear that which is only a reflection? In the naming of the shadow we will take ownership of it and that ownership will bring forth light unto the dark.

WHAT'S POSSIBLE FOR YOU NOW?

Coming down to Earth is not an easy thing to do. It requires a great deal of courage, since most of you forget that you are infinite. To remember this fact is a journey that seems to require so many lifetimes. This is not because you <u>have</u> to live them all to remember but because you harbor so much resistance. But your soul doesn't carry that resistance. You did not enter Earth with it. At some point, you picked it up. This is not generally a conscious decision. You see, this is a game of frequency, and at young ages your frequencies are so much more malleable. As a result, simply by exposure, you entrain into certain belief patterns playing into the collective.

What do you believe would happen if children were born into frequencies of a collective that hasn't forgotten it's infinite potential? Let go of the frequencies you hold, all of them, when the time comes to expand. At every opportunity to feel more deeply, take it, so that you continue to shed the layers of limitations. This process will continue to bring you closer to your truth.

45260945R00042

Made in the USA
San Bernardino, CA
27 July 2019